TAPIRS

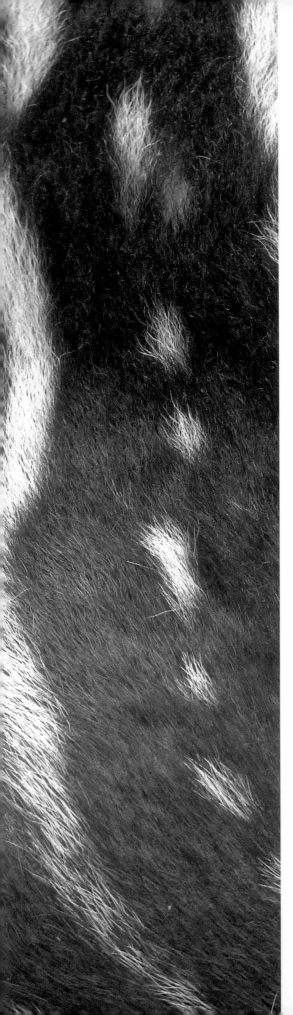

LIVING WILD

Published by Creative Education and Creative Paperbacks
P.O. Box 227, Mankato, Minnesota 56002
Creative Education and Creative Paperbacks are imprints of The Creative Company
www.thecreativecompany.us

Design and production by Mary Herrmann
Art direction by Rita Marshall
Printed in China

Photographs by Alamy (Universal Images Group North America LLC/DeAgostini), Creative Commons Wikimedia (Dante Alighieri, Bluemoose, Brocken Inaglory, Dove, Bernard DUPONT/Flickr, Robert Bruce Horsfall/University of Michigan/Internet Archive, Iconographia Zoologica, International Rhino Foundation/Flickr, Kevmin, Mammalwatcher, Momotarou2012, David Sifry/Flickr), Dreamstime (Enrique David Garcia-salcedo, Marek Jelínek, William Lehman, Le Zhang), iStockphoto (Mark Kostich), Shutterstock (belizar, Uwe Bergwitz, BMJ, dangdumrong, Nick Fox, matthieu Gallet, Glenn R. Specht-grs photo, Jan Gottwald, Ivalin, Ammit Jack, jeep2499, JGA, Tharin kaewkanya, vilena krasnitska, Annika L, mamita, Pedro Helder Pinheiro, Tanya Puntti, tristan tan, TigerStock's, Edward Westmacott, Gosza Wlodarczyk, Wonderly Imaging, Vladimir Wrangel, Yatra, pitchakorn yodmun)

Library of Congress Cataloging-in-Publication Data
Names: Gish, Melissa, author.
Title: Tapirs / Melissa Gish.
Series: Living wild.
Includes bibliographical references and index.
Summary: A look at tapirs, including their habitats, physical characteristics such as their prehensile proboscis, behaviors, relationships with humans, and the vitality of this umbrella species to its forest ecosystem today.
Identifiers: LCCN 2017038416 / ISBN 978-1-60818-962-5 (hardcover) / ISBN 978-1-62832-567-6 (pbk) / ISBN 978-1-64000-041-4 (eBook)

Subjects: LCSH: 1. Tapirs—Juvenile literature. 2. Rare mammals—Juvenile literature.
Classification: LCC QL737.U64 G57 2018 / DDC 599.66—dc23

CCSS: RI.5.1, 2, 3, 8; RST.6-8.1, 2, 5, 6, 8; RH.6-8.3, 4, 5, 6, 7, 8

First Edition HC 9 8 7 6 5 4 3 2 1
First Edition PBK 9 8 7 6 5 4 3 2 1

CREATIVE EDUCATION • CREATIVE PAPERBACKS

TAPIRS

Melissa Gish

In the Brazilian Pantanal, a mother lowland
tapir and her offspring wade through

a marsh, munching tender plants.
A jaguar silently follows them.

In the Brazilian Pantanal, a mother lowland tapir and her offspring wade through a marsh, munching tender plants. A jaguar silently follows them. The breeze shifts, and the mother tapir catches a familiar scent: danger! It is time to move on—and quickly. She squeals and nudges her offspring. The jaguar creeps closer. The tapirs step out of the water onto the spongy shore. Suddenly, the jaguar races forward. The mother tapir turns sharply.

Her offspring squeals and flees into the brush behind her. The jaguar leaps, prepared to crush the mother tapir's skull in its jaws. The tapir ducks at the last moment, and the jaguar catches only a mouthful of fur from the tapir's mane. This jaguar is barely a year old. It has not yet perfected its hunting skills. The tapir bares its sharp teeth and squeals. Deciding this meal is too much trouble, the jaguar retreats into the forest.

WHERE IN THE WORLD THEY LIVE

■ **Baird's Tapir**
forests from
southern Mexico
to northwestern
Colombia

■ **Malayan Tapir**
forests in Myanmar,
Thailand, Malaysia,
and Indonesia

■ **Mountain Tapir**
mountainous forests
from Colombia to
northern Peru

■ **Lowland Tapir**
forests of northern
South America

The four tapir species reside in the thick undergrowth of forested areas as well as in wetlands and mountainous regions. Though tapirs have long been tucked away in such hard-to-reach places, people are gradually taking over, causing tapir population declines ranging from 30 to more than 50 percent since the 1970s. The colored squares represent the areas still inhabited by tapirs in the wild today.

SHY JUNGLE HORSES

The tapir is one of the rarest and least understood large **mammals** in the world. There are four recognized tapir species: Malayan, Baird's, lowland, and mountain. In 2013, a group of scientists announced that a distinct fifth species, the little black tapir, existed, but a year later, another group disagreed, arguing that the little black tapir was a variation of the lowland tapir. The debate continues. Two different pronunciations of the word "tapir" are acceptable: *tay-PEER* and *TAY-pur*. The English word derives from *tapi'ira*, which is the Tupi name for this animal in Brazil. The Malaysian word for tapir is *tenuk*, and in Sumatra, the tapir is called *badak tampung*, which means "having the appearance of a rhinoceros." This name refers to the Sumatran rhinoceros, which is much smaller than the more familiar African and Indian rhinoceroses and has a smaller horn.

In some ways, the tapir does resemble the Sumatran rhino. Tapirs and rhinoceroses are related. Both are members of the order Perissodactyla, a group of animals with an odd number of toes. Tapirs and rhinoceroses have

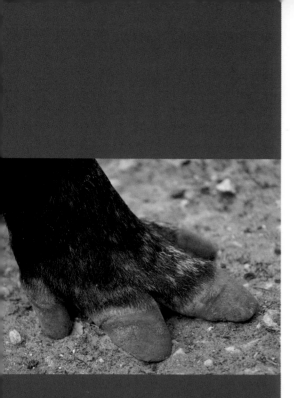

Tapirs' toes spread apart to achieve a better grip, thanks to the leathery skin on the bottoms of their feet.

three toes on the back feet, and rhinos have three toes on the front feet as well; tapirs have four. The two middle toes are larger than the two outer toes and bear most of the animal's weight. More distant tapir relatives include members of the horse family, which have just one toe— the hoof—on each foot. Tapirs are also characterized by a flexible snout, called a proboscis, which is an **adaptation** of the nose and upper lip. It has two nostrils through which the tapir breathes, and it can be used like a curling finger to grasp food and push it into the mouth—like a shortened version of an elephant's trunk. Tapirs are not related to elephants, though tapirs and elephants are the only animals on Earth that possess a functioning proboscis. Males and females share the same coloration and markings, but females can be as much as 20 percent larger than males.

The Malayan tapir, also known as the Asian tapir, is the largest tapir species. It can grow to about eight feet (2.4 m) in length and more than three feet (0.9 m) tall at the shoulder. Large females can weigh up to 1,100 pounds (499 kg), though most weigh roughly 720 pounds (327 kg). The Malayan tapir has a distinctive coat of short, bristly fur. Its head, legs, and body are black except for

When underwater, a tapir can stick
its proboscis out of the water and
breathe through it like a snorkel.

The Malayan tapir's coat pattern breaks up the animal's shape in the eyes of potential predators, an example of disruptive coloration.

a light gray patch that runs from the shoulders to the rump. In this way, Malayan tapirs are said to resemble saddleback pigs. Malayan tapirs were once found in rainforests throughout Southeast Asia but now exist only in scattered areas from southern Myanmar and Thailand to Malaysia and on the Indonesian island of Sumatra. The International Union for Conservation of Nature (IUCN) lists the Malayan tapir as an endangered species and estimates that fewer than 2,000 exist in the wild.

Baird's tapir is named for Spencer Fullerton Baird, an American naturalist who wrote about the tapirs he found in Mexico in 1843. These tapirs range from southern Mexico throughout Central America and along the western side of the Andes Mountains in Colombia. In parts of Mexico, speakers of the Lacandon language, which is derived from ancient Mayan, call them *cash-i-tzimin*. This means "jungle horse." Baird's tapir is the largest land mammal in Central and South America. It averages six feet (1.8 m) in length. Females weigh about 550 pounds (249 kg). Its short fur is solid grayish-brown except for a cream-colored patch covering its cheeks, chin, and throat. Like all tapirs, the tips of its ears are

Though unrelated, domesticated British saddleback pigs and Malayan tapirs share similar coloration.

A study of
lowland tapirs
in Peru once
found seeds from
122 different
plant species in
their dung.

also lightly marked. Although more than twice as many Baird's tapirs as Malayan tapirs are believed to exist, this species is also listed as endangered because its population is steadily decreasing.

Lowland tapirs are about the same size as Baird's, but these animals are solid brown with a stiff mane of bristly fur running from the center of the shoulders to the forehead. Although it has been **extirpated** from much of its range, the lowland tapir is the most widespread of the tapir species. Known also as the Brazilian tapir, it can be found in much of Brazil's Amazon basin and east of the Andes from Colombia to northern Argentina. Researchers cannot estimate the number of lowland tapirs that exist in the wild because these shy animals inhabit areas of the rainforest that are difficult to reach. The IUCN lists the lowland tapir as vulnerable, which means it could become endangered if threats to its survival and reproduction are not reduced. Unrelenting **deforestation** of the Amazon rainforest and increased hunting for wild meat are major threats to lowland tapirs.

The smallest of the tapirs is the mountain tapir. Also called the woolly tapir, it is known for its long, dense

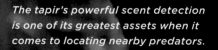

The tapir's powerful scent detection is one of its greatest assets when it comes to locating nearby predators.

Cloud forests are located at higher elevations than rainforests, resulting in cooler and more humid climates.

Tapirs do not really swim; they sink down and walk across the muddy bottoms of lakes, rivers, and flooded wetlands.

fur, which is dark brown or black. It has a distinctive white rim around its lips. Though its body is about as long and tall as the Baird's and lowland tapirs, it ranges in size from about 350 pounds (159 kg) for males up to about 500 pounds (227 kg) for females. Mountain tapirs can be found only in the Andes of Colombia, Ecuador, and northwestern Peru, at elevations up to about 13,000 feet (3,962 m). They inhabit cloud forests, which are characterized by near-constant cool, misty conditions, as well as high, treeless grasslands called the páramo. This species is also listed as endangered. Scientists believe that fewer than 2,500 mountain tapirs remain in the wild.

All tapirs have sharp teeth that are used mainly for defense against predators. They have few natural enemies, but wild cats such as jaguars, margays, and ocelots sometimes target their young. Tapirs' eyesight is myopic, meaning they cannot clearly see objects in the distance. They make up for this with excellent hearing and a strong sense of smell. If they sense danger, tapirs run and hide in thick brush. They may also submerge underwater, breathing through their proboscis like a snorkel, until the threat has passed.

Rivers, lakes, and swamps are essential to tapir habitats, both for food sources and for protection from predators.

Tapirs use their sharp molars to snap small saplings and grind thick leaves and tough twigs into a pulpy mash.

GARDENERS OF THE FOREST

dult tapirs were believed to be **solitary** animals, but recent studies have found they sometimes graze in pairs or small groups. They establish home ranges where they live and forage for food. These areas vary from less than half a square mile to nearly 10 square miles (1.3–25.9 sq km). Tapirs mark the boundaries of their home ranges by spraying urine on plants and trees and travel regularly along paths that they have established. They do not, however, defend their home range against other tapirs. They generally ignore one another. All but the mountain tapir are nocturnal, or active at night. During much of the day, they hide in thick patches of underbrush and sleep. In late afternoon, they wake and begin browsing. Mountain tapirs are diurnal, which means they are more active during the day. All tapirs are herbivores. They eat only plant matter—up to 85 pounds (38.6 kg) per day. They nibble twigs and buds, munch on shoots and leaves, and submerge underwater to pluck plants from the mud. They eat berries and fallen fruit and may even push trees with their bodies to make fruit drop to the ground.

Captive tapirs are fed a variety of fruit and plant material and are sometimes given sugar-rich bananas and apples as treats.

Tapirs are not aggressive, but their teeth can become weapons if the animals need to defend themselves.

With a long and flexible snout, the tapir can graze on a circle of land 12 inches (30.5 cm) in diameter without turning its head.

The tapir's diverse diet and short digestive system have earned this animal the nickname "gardener of the forest." Tapirs eat on the go, dropping undigested seeds in their **dung**—often far from where the original plant or tree grew. The seeds sprout directly from the tapir's dung, which acts like a packet of natural fertilizer to help the new plants and trees grow. Animals that modify their habitats in such a way are called **ecosystem** engineers. They help shape and influence the health of their environment. Tapirs are also considered an umbrella species. This means that their actions affect the lives of many other species beneath them on the **food chain**. Tapirs are vital to the success of their ecosystem.

Adult tapirs have 42 to 44 teeth. Like their browsing relatives, rhinoceroses and horses, tapirs have sharp front teeth, called incisors, suited to clipping grass close to the ground. Their back teeth, called molars, are sharply ridged for grinding food into a pulp. Unlike their relatives, though, tapirs also have two sharp canine teeth in the lower jaw and two shorter canines in the upper jaw. These are used for defense. Because of their size, adult tapirs face few natural dangers. While swimming, Malayan

tapirs may fall prey to large crocodiles, and in the dense rainforest, tigers and leopards may attack if smaller prey is not available. In the **Neotropics**, jaguars are a potential threat in the rainforest, and cougars are known to attack mountain tapirs. Baby tapirs, called calves, are common targets of predators, including large cats, crocodile-like reptiles called caimans, and even anacondas. When calves are threatened, they do not run away as many young mammals do. Rather, they hide near their mother and let her defend them with her sharp teeth. Tapirs' jaws

Baby tapirs' coloration provides camouflage, helping the calves blend in with their surroundings.

Typically, animals that take a long time to produce and raise their young are more protective of their offspring.

are powerful and can inflict serious wounds. Defensive mother tapirs can be vicious if threatened.

Little is known about tapir reproduction in the wild. Because tapirs are nocturnal and elusive, researchers find it difficult to follow them. Much of what is known about tapir reproduction comes from captive tapirs in zoos. Tapirs are old enough to mate when they are two to three years old. Male tapirs are called bulls, and females are called cows. Malayan tapirs typically breed in May or June, but other tapirs can breed at any time of year. Tapirs use scent to locate each other in the forest. Males attracted to the same female may fight over her, biting each other until one backs down and runs away. The winner of the challenge approaches the female and begins courtship. The tapirs sniff one another. They make wheezing and whistling sounds as they walk circles around each other. The mating encounter is brief, ending when the female chases away the male. The female remains on her own during the long **gestation** of 13 to 14 months.

Female tapirs give birth standing up. One calf is born. Twins are extremely rare. Calves do not resemble their parents right away. Their soft fur is dark brown or black with yellow or white stripes and spots that resemble the markings on a watermelon. This coat helps the calf blend in with grasses and shrubs. Calves weigh between 7 and 25 pounds (3.2–11.3 kg), depending on the species. They are born with their eyes open and can walk within a few hours of birth. They depend on their mother's **nutrient**-rich milk, nursing two or three times a day. Calves are born without teeth, but within two weeks, their first

Malayan tapirs breed well in zoos, but producing only one baby every few years makes the process slow.

The San Diego Zoo began a Malayan tapir breeding program in 1940, with more than 30 calves born since then.

Subadults may continue to forage with their mother beyond 18 months of age.

chisel-shaped front teeth erupt and they begin nibbling at vegetation alongside their mother. Later, their sharp, pointed canines and wide cheek teeth will grow. Calves lose their markings and take on their adult coloration when they are about six months old. They may continue to supplement their diet with their mother's milk until they are one year old. Now they are called subadults and will continue to grow for about another six months until they reach their adult size. They will remain with their mothers an additional six months or until their mothers give birth again. Fully grown and no longer in need of their mothers' protection, young tapirs will wander away from their mothers and begin life on their own.

Tapirs have remained alive in captivity for more than 30 years, and captive females have given birth well into their 20s. It is believed that wild tapirs have equally long life spans. But because their reproductive cycle is so long— females may have only one calf every two to three years— the loss of even one tapir can have damaging effects on the entire population. As tapir numbers dwindle, the danger of **inbreeding** increases. Without sufficient **genetic** diversity, tapirs could soon become **extinct**.

A mother tapir is on constant alert for approaching danger, and her youngster never strays far from her side.

When scientists first named the Malayan tapir in 1819, they dubbed the species maiba, which means "different" in Malay.

1/8 de la grand-nat-

Werner. del.

Fr. Cuvier M

Lithog

Maïba mâle

DREAM EATERS AND SWAMP MONSTERS

In Caracas, Venezuela, is a statue of María Lionza, a beloved native goddess of nature and animals, riding a tapir.

T apirs have been part of cultural history for thousands of years. When the first civilizations arose more than 4,000 years ago in the Andes of Peru, shamans became the spiritual and medical advisers of their people. Shamans believed that because tapirs had only three toes on their hind feet—different from other animals—the tapir's feet had special power. To this day, tapirs are used in traditional folk medicine. The Kallawaya are descendants of the doctors of 12th- and 13th-century Inca rulers. Today, the Kallawaya continue to work as traditional healers in the Andes of Bolivia. They use tapir toenails and feet in medicine and consider tapir bones, teeth, and hides good-luck charms.

Around 500 B.C., a tapir **cult** grew among the Huari people, who existed in Peru until about A.D. 1000. Because tapirs were silent and seemed to disappear into the forest, shamans saw them as keepers of secret wisdom spoken to them by the spirit world. They believed some people shared the tapir's gift. Epilepsy is a brain disorder that can cause people to have **convulsions**. During these convulsions, saliva may turn frothy and white,

As Central and South America's largest native land mammal, Baird's tapir can often hold its own against a jaguar.

In southern Mexico, the Baird's tapir is called *anteburro* ("small donkey"), and in Belize, it is the "mountain cow."

spilling onto the lips. This reminded the people of the white markings around the mountain tapir's mouth. Shamans did not understand epilepsy. They thought that convulsions and frothy mouths were the results of a person transforming into a mountain tapir, so epileptics were believed to be divine beings.

Archaeologist J. Scott Raymond, on an expedition to Peru in 1967, found evidence of the tapir cult on a piece of Huari pottery—a cup in the shape of a tapir's left foot. Painted on the cup was the image of a bird twisted in an unnatural pose. Because birds were symbolic of the spirit world, Raymond's team believed the bird represented an epileptic person having a convulsion. The connection between tapirs and epilepsy persisted for hundreds of years, becoming part of the medicine practiced in the Inca Empire beginning in the early 13th century.

When Spanish explorers reached South America in the 16th century, they believed epilepsy was a terrible disease. Thinking the tapir's feet provided protection from epilepsy, the Spanish explorers took the animal's feet back to Europe. A tapir toe was held in the left hand and then inserted into the left ear, or a piece of the toe was

made into a ring that was worn on the left hand. A foot could be rubbed on the chest or worn on a string around the neck. Sometimes the toenails were crushed and consumed in a tea. When the Spanish destroyed the Incan civilization in the 1570s, the tapir cult and its mysticism faded from memory.

One tapir legend persists to this day. A mysterious beast called the *tapirê-iauara* is said to inhabit the Amazon floodplain. People who claim to have seen it describe it as

Similar to North America's bison, mountain tapirs have thick hides and dense fur to survive the cooler climate of the Andes.

FROM CHAPTER IV

The noblest and most generally pursued game is the anta (tapir), that representative of the pachyderms in the New World, which, in the Old, is found at only a few places in India. It flourishes in extraordinary numbers, yet does not herd together in troops, on the densely wooded shores of all the tributaries of the Amazon and La Plata. All the narrow gorges and moist ravines, clad with rich vegetation, and the forests on the shores of murmuring rivulets, and near the roaring cataracts of large rivers, are sure to shelter that diminutive of the elephant. At early dawn, it leaves its quiet nook behind thorny bambusaceæ, or leafy bushes, and walks gravely to the river by deeply trodden paths of its own engineering, for it thoroughly enjoys a cold bath in the morning; and often, when quickly doubling some sharp bend in the river, we surprised it sitting in quiet majesty up to the neck in the water. It swims and dives with astonishing agility; and it may be the sense of greater security in the aqueous element, ... which impels it always to take the shortest cut to the river when pursued by the dogs....

Only the female anta, with her young one, never flies before the dogs. She remains courageously in her retreat, endeavouring to protect with her own body the trembling little creature that creeps between her legs, and vents its anxiety in shrill whistling sounds. Woe to the hardy cur that dares ... to come within reach of the grim dam. Her elevated short jaw bares some teeth that demand respect, and under her powerful forelegs the weak ribs of a dog would snap like thin reeds.

excerpt from The Amazon and Madeira Rivers, *by Franz Keller (1835–90)*

being the size of a cow, with the body and face of a tapir and the claws and teeth of a jaguar. In the early 1980s, Dr. Nigel J. H. Smith, a geographer conducting research in the Amazon, collected an amazing story from a local fisherman. The man and his friend were fishing at night in a flooded forest near the Tapajós River when they decided to hang up their hammocks and nap. Suddenly, a tapirê-iauara leaped out of the water and grabbed his friend right out of his hammock. The beast dragged him underwater and disappeared. He was never seen again. Many people in Brazil swear that the tapirê-iauara is real—just like many people in North America swear that Bigfoot is real.

On the other side of the world, the Malayan tapir was part of a very different tradition. In Thailand, the tapir is called *p'somm-sett*, which means "mixture is finished." This refers to the ancient Thai belief that tapirs were constructed from pieces that were left over when the Creator made all the other animals. In Malaysia, the Orang Asli, an **indigenous** people, have a different idea of how the tapir came to look the way it does. According to their folklore, the tapir once had a long horn like the rhinoceros, sharp teeth like the tiger, and a beautiful black

Though typically nocturnal, tapirs have been spotted cooling down and feeding at water sources during the day.

Tapirs like to wallow in pools of mud, protecting their bodies against pesky biting insects and ticks.

Tapirs can curl their flexible proboscis all the way inside their mouth.

The lowland tapir was nearly extinct in Bolivia before the creation of Madidi National Park in 1995.

coat like the panther. Although he was handsome, he was also vain and mean. The other animals grew weary of the tapir's constant boasting, so one day, the mice made a potion of herbs and flowers that made the tapir fall asleep. While he slept, the mice sawed off his horn, filed down his teeth, and covered his coat with mud and ashes from a firepit. When the tapir awoke, he found that his head was bare, his teeth were stubs, and he had an ashen gray patch over a dull coat. Horrified, he ran into the forest, where, to this day, he hides and never speaks.

The tapir has also become attached to a creature from Japanese **mythology** called Baku, who is known as the eater of nightmares. Baku emerged sometime between the 14th and 15th centuries as a mash-up of many different animals. It originally had a bear's body, a tiger's feet, and an elephant's trunk, with a rhinoceros's eyes and an ox's tail. The story is that if children called its name three times, it would come to their bedside and gobble up their nightmares, helping them return to sleep. In Chinese and Korean folklore, the Baku appeared with a shortened trunk so it looked more like a tapir. In modern times, the Baku has evolved completely into a

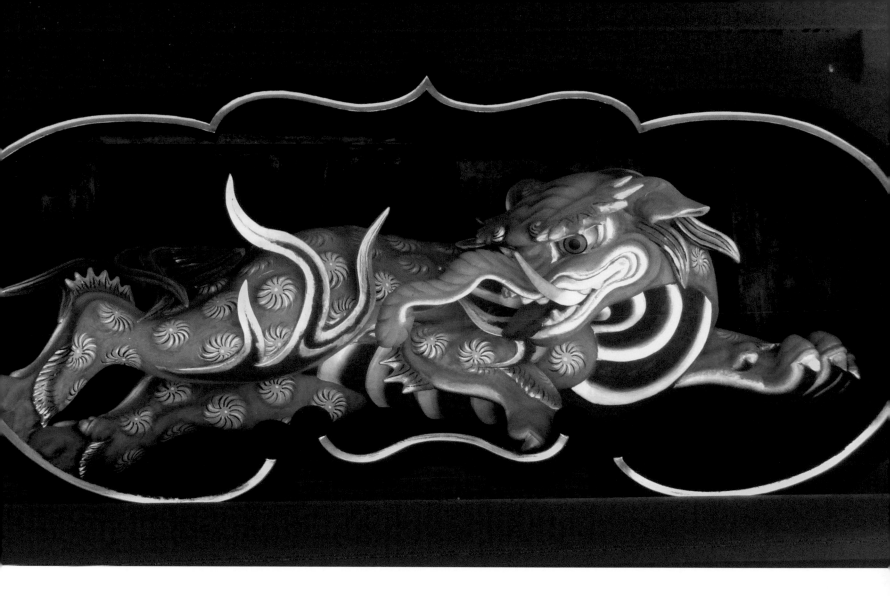

tapir. Mamoru Oshii's 1984 anime film, *Urusei Yatsura 2: Beautiful Dreamer,* depicted Baku as a Malayan tapir. In the world of Pokémon, Drowzee is a Baku who looks similar to a tapir. The story of Drowzee tells that if a person gets an itchy nose while sleeping, it could be Drowzee trying to eat a bad dream. And in the Digimon universe, Tapirmon is a dream-eater that looks like a tapir with tusks. It wears a special ring on its foreleg that marks it as a holy species.

In Japanese folklore, if Baku is not satisfied after eating nightmares, he may also eat a person's hopes and dreams!

The earliest tapir relative, Heptodon, had a fat upper lip instead of the prehensile snout of modern tapirs.

LIVING FOSSILS IN THE FOREST

 bout 50 million years ago, when North America was hot and humid like a jungle, the earliest tapirs were small. Fossils of a species in the genus *Heptodon* were found in British Columbia in 2014. These show that early tapir ancestors were about half as big as modern lowland tapirs. Similar teeth and bones of another tapir ancestor were found near the North Pole on Canada's Ellesmere Island. By about 30 million years ago, tapirs grew bigger. *Protapirus obliquidens* existed in what is today the Great Plains. The fossilized remains of a partial skull were first collected in 1894 in South Dakota by fossil hunter H. F. Wells. *Protapirus obliquidens* was about the same size as modern tapirs, and its teeth suggest that it was also an herbivore. About 10 million years after *Protapirus obliquidens*, another tapir emerged on the Great Plains. It was *Miotapirus harrisonensis*, and it also looked almost the same as the tapirs we know today.

As the last Ice Age began about 1.8 million years ago, many animals grew quite large. They included mammoths, mastodons, ground sloths, saber-toothed cats, and even a beaver that grew nine feet (2.7 m) long. But tapirs stayed

Celebrated on April 27th, World Tapir Day seeks to increase awareness of tapirs and raise funds for tapir conservation in South America.

The ridges on the teeth of Tapirus veroensis *indicate that it chomped twigs rather than ate grass.*

mostly the same. Only a few grew as large as the biggest modern tapirs. They included the 600-pound (272 kg) *Tapirus veroensis*, which lived in the southeastern United States, and Asia's *Megatapirus augustus*, or giant tapir. The giant tapir weighed about 1,100 pounds (499 kg). *Tapirus veroensis* and three other North American tapir species died out roughly 11,000 years ago, leaving the three Neotropic species we know today. **Subfossil** discoveries in southern China and Vietnam show that the giant tapir existed until 4,000 years ago, leaving the Malayan tapir as Asia's only tapir species. Scientists consider tapirs to be "living fossils" because they have remained virtually unchanged from their prehistoric ancestors.

For tens of millions of years, tapirs experienced shifting continents, changing climates, and other natural events that drastically affected their habitats. Through it all, tapirs survived. But today, tapirs face a threat more powerful than any they've previously endured: humans. Tapirs are relentlessly hunted for their meat. Escape is nearly impossible. During the past 40 years, close to 20 percent of the Amazon rainforest has been cut down. That is more destruction than throughout the previous

450 years since Europeans first arrived in South America. More than 90 percent of Brazil's Atlantic coastal forests have disappeared. And nearly half of the Pantanal—the world's largest tropical wetland—has been drained and converted for agriculture and other human use. Tapirs simply have nowhere to go.

Species conservation plans require information about animals' behaviors, habits, reproduction, and roles in their ecosystems. Until recently, very little was known about tapirs, so conservation measures were practically

Huge swaths of Central and South American rainforests are destroyed daily to make way for the expansion of agriculture.

Tapirs cut paths and use them to regularly travel through their forest and marshy grassland habitats.

nonexistent. In 1996, Brazilian wildlife **ecologist** Dr. Patrícia Medici decided to make tapirs her life's work. She started the Atlantic Forest Tapir Program, which began collecting data on tapir biology, health, genetics, habitat use, and the effects of habitat **fragmentation**. The program also led community education in **sustainability** and habitat restoration projects. Today, Dr. Medici's program has expanded. She is the head of the Lowland Tapir Conservation Initiative, which organizes research and education programs aimed at creating tapir conservation plans throughout Brazil. One such activity is the Pantanal Tapir Program. It puts researchers in the field to track and study elusive tapirs.

A variety of strategies are employed to study tapirs in their natural environment. Motion-activated cameras capable of night vision are used to document tapirs' nocturnal feeding, mating, and reproductive behaviors. Tapirs are also shot with tranquilizer darts to make them fall asleep. While the tapir is asleep, the team takes measurements and collects hair and blood samples for genetic identification. Then a collar holding a **Global Positioning System** (GPS) tracking device is fitted around the tapir's neck. The GPS transmitter allows Medici's team to monitor the tapir's movements. The collar also has reflective tape on it. Tapirs are frequently hit by vehicles at night. Medici hopes the tape will help make tapirs more visible on roadways so that drivers can avoid collisions.

Similar research programs have emerged in recent years. In 2002, Denmark's Copenhagen Zoo, in partnership with Malaysia's Department of Wildlife and National Parks, conducted a study of Malayan tapirs. Researchers put radio collars on five tapirs but almost immediately lost contact with two of the animals.

Female tapirs tend to range more widely than male tapirs, but all tapirs typically avoid humans.

Tapirs rarely gather together, but when they do, the group of tapirs is called a candle.

When a tapir raises its snout and curls its lips, it is flehmening, or capturing scent via the Jacobson's organ in its mouth.

Studying animals that hide in such dense forests is exceedingly difficult. Results of the study showed promise, however, and the Copenhagen Zoo helped fund the Malay Tapir Conservation Center in Malaysia's Sungai Dusun Wildlife Reserve. Here, captive tapirs are bred and orphaned wild tapirs are raised. The facility was originally created for the Sumatran rhino, but that animal was declared extinct in Malaysia in 2015. Now the facility is being used to try to save the Malayan tapir by breeding and rehabilitating tapirs and then releasing them into the wild. Released tapirs are fitted with GPS collars so that researchers can track the animals and determine whether reintroduction efforts are successful.

Nai Conservation studies tapir movement and land use in Costa Rica. In 2015, with help from the London Zoological Society, Nai Conservation launched a program to study the effects of vehicle collisions on Baird's tapir populations. Researchers set up dozens of remote cameras in the forests surrounding various highways. They also study the ecology and genetics of tapirs in the Cordillera de Talamanca, a mountain range bordering Costa Rica and Panama. The least understood

tapir species is the mountain tapir. Researchers at the Universidad de los Andes, in Bogotá, Colombia, teamed up with scientists from the United Kingdom's University of Kent to study mountain tapirs. They also used GPS collars as their main strategy in studying tapirs. Their goal was to learn about tapir distribution throughout their habitats and how they interacted with their environments. As long as dedicated researchers from around the world continue to work together to uncover the secrets of tapirs and develop successful conservation plans, these amazing animals just might have a chance of avoiding extinction.

Because tapirs' fur is short, they must seek out shade or wallow in mud to protect their skin against sunburn.

ANIMAL TALE: HOW TAPIR GIRL BECAME EARTH

The Bribrí are an indigenous people of southern Costa Rica and northern Panama. Their tradition of living off the land has continued to this day. Similarly, their mythology has endured over many generations. This Bribrí myth describes the people's relationship to the tapir.

Sibú is the creator of all things. He lives in Suláyum, the center of the world. One day, Sibú decided to create Earth's soil. He thought the blood of a perfect being should become the earth, so he sent Vampire Bat over the sunrise to find a perfect being.

Vampire Bat flew over the sunrise and found one of the spirits who had helped build Suláyum. He bit the spirit and drank some of its blood. Then Vampire Bat flew back to Sibú, who was resting in his hammock. Vampire Bat left some droppings, which instantly turned to dust and blew away. Sibú could see that this being was not perfect. It could not be used to make earth. So Sibú ordered Vampire Bat to fly under the sunset in search of a perfect being.

Vampire Bat flew under the sunset and found SuLa, who guards the underworld and is Sibú's sister. Sitting beside SuLa was her daughter, Iriria, a tapir girl. Vampire Bat bit Iriria and drank some of her blood. Then he flew back to Sibú, who was waiting under the moon. Vampire Bat left some droppings. Instantly, green vines and trees sprouted from Vampire Bat's droppings. Sibú could see that Vampire Bat had found a perfect being that could be used to make earth.

Sibú sent out a decree that everyone should gather at Suláyum for a great festival. He would create earth and grow the first people from it. But he kept this intention to himself, for the spirits who had helped build Suláyum would be jealous if they had to share the world with people. Moreover, SuLa would be angry if she knew what Sibú had planned for Iriria the tapir girl.

Everyone came to the festival—the spirits who had helped build Suláyum as well as Bikakra, who was the first grandmother, and SuLa with her daughter Iriria. To begin, Sibú asked Bikakra to perform the chocolate ceremony. Chocolate was the symbol of blood and the making of all life. After Bikakra gave chocolate to everyone, a special dance called the Sorbón began. The spirits danced. SuLa danced. And Iriria the tapir girl danced.

Then Sibú whispered into Vampire Bat's ear. The time had come. Vampire Bat sneaked up behind Iriria as she danced and bit her. Blood began to flow from the girl's leg. Everyone continued to dance the Sorbón, unaware of what Vampire Bat had done to Iriria. Soon, the poor tapir girl collapsed. Sibú began to dance on Iriria's body, crushing it to fine bits until the tapir girl became earth.

Suddenly, green trees and vines sprouted from this new earth. Sibú scattered kernels of corn in the earth. The corn grew into the first people. SuLa was heartbroken that her brother had taken Iriria and turned her into earth. She made the people promise to never eat tapirs except at special chocolate festivals that celebrate the sacrifice of Iriria the tapir girl. Today, the Bribrí people still honor the tapir as a sacred animal.

adaptation – a change in a species that helps it survive in a changed environment

archaeologist – a person who studies human history by examining ancient peoples and their artifacts

convulsions – sudden jerking movements of limbs or the body, caused by involuntary tightening of muscles

cult – a group of people who worship a particular figure or object

deforestation – the clearing away of trees from a forest

dung – waste matter eliminated from the body of an animal

ecologist – a person who studies the relationships of organisms living together in an environment

ecosystem – a community of organisms that live together in an environment

extinct – having no living members

extirpated – made to cease to exist in a certain place

food chain – a system in nature in which living things are dependent on each other for food

fragmentation – the breaking up of an organism's habitat into scattered sections that may result in difficulty moving safely from one place to another

genetic – relating to genes, the basic physical units of heredity

gestation – the period of time it takes a baby to develop inside its mother's womb

Global Positioning System – a system of satellites, computers, and other electronic devices that work together to determine the location of objects or living things that carry a trackable device

inbreeding – the mating of individuals that are closely related; it can result in having offspring with health problems

indigenous – originating in a particular region or country

mammals – warm-blooded animals that have a backbone and hair or fur, give birth to live young, and produce milk to feed their young

mythology – a collection of myths, or popular, traditional beliefs or stories that explain how something came to be or that are associated with a person or object

Neotropics – the geographical region (especially pertaining to the species found therein) that includes South and Central America, the southern Mexican lowlands, the Caribbean Islands, and southern Florida

nutrient – a substance that gives a living thing energy and helps it grow

solitary – alone, without companions

subfossil – the remains of an animal that have not become completely fossilized, or turned to rock

sustainability – the ability to be renewed or kept functioning

SELECTED BIBLIOGRAPHY

"All About the Terrific Tapir." Tapir Specialist Group. http://tapirs.org/tapirs/.

Macdonald, David W., ed. *The Princeton Encyclopedia of Mammals*. Princeton, N.J.: Princeton University Press, 2009.

Medici, Patrícia. "The Coolest Animal You Know Nothing About and How We Can Save It." TED Talk. https://www.ted.com/talks/patricia_medici_the_coolest_animal_you_know_nothing_about_and_how_we_can_save_it.

"Tapir." San Diego Zoo Animals & Plants. http://animals.sandiegozoo.org/animals/tapir.

Wells, Jeffrey. "*Tapirus bairdii*—Baird's Tapir." Animal Diversity Web. http://animaldiversity.org/accounts/Tapirus_bairdii/.

Yong Hoi Sen, ed. *Animals*. Vol. 3 of *Encyclopedia of Malaysia*. Singapore: Editions Didier Millet, 2007.

Note: Every effort has been made to ensure that any websites listed above were active at the time of publication. However, because of the nature of the Internet, it is impossible to guarantee that these sites will remain active indefinitely or that their contents will not be altered.

Endangered because of human activity, tapirs must now rely on people to protect their remaining populations.